SATIVACOIN

COMMODITY DRIVEN CRYPTO

2014-2015-2016
A CONCISE SATIVACOIN HISTORY BOOK

Sativacoin—Commodity Driven Crypto

by Christopher P. Thompson

Book Author by Christopher P. Thompson

Book Design by C. Ellis

ISBN—13: 978-1973719373
ISBN—10: 1973719371

SATIVACOIN

COMMODITY DRIVEN CRYPTO

2014—2015—2016
A CONCISE SATIVACOIN HISTORY BOOK

CHRISTOPHER P. THOMPSON

CONTENTS

Introduction 8-9

What is Sativacoin? 10
Why use Sativacoin? 11
Is Sativacoin Money? 12
Coin Specification 13
Milestone Timeline 14-15
Top Shelf Toker 16
Proof of Work (PoW) Mining 17
Blockchain 18
Block Time 19
Cryptocurrency Exchanges 20
Community 21

A Concise History of Sativacoin 23

1   Launch of the Sativacoin Blockchain 24-29
2   Takeover of Sativacoin by the Altcoin.center 30-33
3   Sativacoin Rebranded and Hard Forked 34-39
4   All Time High 2016 Market Capitalisation 40-45
5   Third Sativacoin Bitcointalk Thread Created 46-49

INTRODUCTION

Since the inception of Bitcoin in 2008, thousands of cryptocurrencies or decentralised blockchains have been launched. Most ventures into the crypto sphere have not gone to plan as their founders would have hoped. Nevertheless, there are currently hundreds of crypto related projects which are succeeding.

This book covers the history of Sativacoin, an open-source, publicly accessible blockchain, from the 21st September 2014 to the end of 2016. During that time, the project was rescued in late 2014 (original lead developer left) and the blockchain was hard forked in March 2015. Since that time, development has been ongoing. Major topics covered in this book include:

- Sativacoin blockchain was launched (September 2014)

- Sativacoin was added to www.coinmarketcap.com (October 2014)

- Arnel Larracas entered the community (October 2014)

- Altcoin.center took over the project (November 2014)

- Second official Sativacoin Bitcointalk thread created (November 2014)

- Sativacoin network protocol hard forked (March 2015)

- Bittrex terminated active trading of STV/BTC (July 2015)

- Bittrex reactivated active trading of STV/BTC (November 2015)

- CoinGecko began to statistically rank Sativacoin (January 2016)

- Coinpayments.net began to accept STV (April 2016)

- All time high 2016 market capitalisation attained (September 2016)

- Third official Sativacoin Bitcointalk thread created (September 2016)

INTRODUCTION

This book covers twenty eight (28) months, contained within five chapters, of historical events in chronological order.

During the year 2017, the project has shifted from being primarily focused on cannabis to commodities in general.

You may have bought this book because Sativacoin is your favourite cryptographic blockchain. Alternatively, you may be keen to find out how it all began. I have presented the information henceforth without going into too much technical discussion about Sativacoin. If you would like to investigate further, I recommend that you read material currently available online at the official website at https://www.sativacoin.io.

If you choose to purchase a certain amount of STV, please do not buy more than you can afford to lose.

Enjoy the book :D

WHAT IS SATIVACOIN?

Sativacoin is a cryptocurrency or digital decentralised currency used via the Internet. It is described as a payment network without the need for a central authority such as a bank or other central clearing house. It allows the end user to store or transfer value anywhere in the world with the use of a personal computer, laptop or smartphone. Cryptography has been implemented and coded into the network allowing the user to send currency through a decentralised (no centre point of failure), open source (anyone can review the code), peer-to-peer network. Cryptography also controls the creation of newly mined/minted STV.

It was announced on the 21st September 2014 by an anonymous individual or group known as user "sativacoin". It was originally a hybrid proof of work/stake cryptocurrency, but became solely proof of stake on the 26th September 2014.

One month after the blockchain was launched, Arnel Larracas (a Filipino American) became involved with the project. He has regularly stated his devotion to make Sativacoin a high profile cryptocurrency within the space.

During the next few years, he has plans to grow Sativacoin. Some key aims going forward include:

- To develop and release mobile wallet clients (Android/IOS)

- To establish an independent Sativacoin Foundation and forum

- To get the coin listed on Poloniex (a major exchange)

- To attract as much media attention as possible

The slogan used by Sativacoin to market their cryptocurrency is:

"Cryptocurrency Built For Commodities"

WHY USE SATIVACOIN?

Like all cryptocurrencies, people have chosen to adopt Sativacoin as a medium of exchange through personal choice. An innovative feature of the coin, an affinity towards the brand or high confidence in the community could be reasons why they have done so. Key benefits of using Sativacoin are:

- It is a useful medium of exchange via which value can be transferred internationally for a fraction of the cost of other conventional methods.

- Sativacoin eliminates the need for a trusted third party such as a bank, clearing house or other centralised authority (e.g. PayPal). All transactions are solely from one person to another (peer-to-peer).

- Sativacoin has the potential to engage people worldwide who are without a bank account (unbanked).

- Sativacoin is immune from the effects of hyperinflation, unlike the current fiat monetary systems around the world.

IS SATIVACOIN MONEY?

Money is a form of acceptable, convenient and valued medium of payment for goods and services within an economy. It allows two parties to exchange goods or services without the need to barter. This eradicates the potential situation where one party of the two may not want what the other has to offer. The main properties of money are:

- **As a medium of exchange**—money can be used as a means to buy/sell goods/services without the need to barter.

- **A unit of account**—a common measure of value wherever one is in the world.

- **Portable**—easily transferred from one party to another. The medium used can be easily carried.

- **Durable**—all units of the currency can be lost, but not destroyed.

- **Divisible**—each unit can be subdivided into smaller fractions of that unit.

- **Fungible**— each unit of account is the same as every other unit within the medium (1 STV= 1 STV).

- **As a store of value**—it sustains its purchasing power (what it can buy) over long periods of time.

Sativacoin easily satisfies the first six characteristics. Taking into account the last characteristic, the value of Sativacoin, like all currencies, comes from people willing to accept it as a medium of exchange for payment of goods or services. As it gets adopted by more individuals or merchants, its intrinsic value will increase accordingly.

COIN SPECIFICATION

Since the birth of Sativacoin, its coin specification has changed a few times. At the time of publication of this book, its current specification is:

Coin Symbol:	STV
Unit of account:	STV
Date of Announcement:	21st of September 2014 at 16:40:08 UTC
Block Number One Generated:	21st of September 2014 at 16:09:57 UTC
Date of Launch:	21st of September 2014
Founder:	user "sativacoin"
Hashing Algorithms:	X-13
Last Proof of Work Block:	7,200
Timestamping Algorithm:	Proof of Stake
Proof of Stake Interest:	5%
Minimum Stake Age:	24 hours
Maximum Stake Age:	None
Address Begins With:	S
Total Coins:	10 million
Block Time:	60 seconds (average)
Coins per Block:	972 per PoW block (7,200 PoW blocks)
Pre-mine:	9 blocks (9*972) or 0.125% of PoW coins

MILESTONE TIMELINE

21st September 2014	—Block number one timestamped at 16:09:57 UTC
21st September 2014	—Sativacoin announced on Bitcointalk at 16:40:08 UTC
22nd September 2014	—Coinbroker initiated STV/BTC the trading pair
22nd September 2014	—C-Cex initiated the STV/BTC trading pair
23rd September 2014	—Bittrex initiated the STV/BTC trading pair
25th September 2014	—Original lead developer abandoned the coin
26th September 2014	—PoW mining phase ended at block number 7,200
20th October 2014	—Sativacoin added to www.coinmarketcap.com
22nd October 2014	—Arnel Larracas posted his first comment on the official Sativacoin Bitcointalk forum thread
26th November 2014	—Sativacoin announced as taken over at 13:06:01 UTC and a new Sativacoin Bitcointalk thread created.
6th January 2015	—ALTS.trade initiated the STV/BTC trading pair
14th March 2015	—Sativacoin network protocol hard forked
15th March 2015	—New official Facebook account founded
20th March 2015	—http://blockexperts.com/stv went live
20th April 2015	—Worldwide celebration of cannabis consumption
19th July 2015	—Bittrex terminated the STV/BTC trading pair
21st September 2015	—First year anniversary of the coin
17th November 2015	—YoBit initiated the STV/BTC trading pair
18th November 2015	—Bittrex reinstated the STV/BTC trading pair
10th December 2015	—Cryptopia initiated the STV/BTC trading pair
16th December 2015	—Cryptocloud Hosting began to accept Sativacoin

MILESTONE TIMELINE

3rd January 2016	—Coingather initiated the STV/BTC trading pair
5th January 2016	—CoinGecko began to statistically rank Sativacoin
19th January 2016	—alcurEX initiated the STV/BTC trading pair
20th April 2016	—Coinpayments.net began to accept STV as a form of payment for merchant services
22nd April 2016	—Novaexchange initiated the STV/BTC trading pair
27th April 2016	—Pex Pepper became the first Coinpayments.net merchant to accept payment using STV
8th May 2016	—Cryptopia initiated the STV/ETH trading pair
1st September 2016	—All time high 2016 market capitalisation of approximately US$169,861 attained
21st September 2016	—Second year anniversary of the coin
26th September 2016	—Third Bitcointalk thread created for Sativacoin at 02:45:39 UTC
27th September 2016	—https://chainz.cryptoid.info/stv/ went live
13th October 2016	—Highest daily trading volume of Sativacoin was recorded at 5.85 BTC
31st December 2016	—Last block of 2016 timestamped at 23:59:44 UTC

TOP SHELF TOKER

Top Shelf Toker is a clothing company based out of Chicago, Illinois. Our company is catered to everyone from the everyday enthusiast to the cannabis connoisseur. We strive to provide our customers with quality apparel at an affordable price. Shop our hats, tees, buttons, and much more to show your support and help us spread the message of the Top Shelf Toker Movement!

Top Shelf Toker embodies much more than just a clothing brand. At Top Shelf Toker we know that the utility of hemp, cannabis, and cryptocurrency is more than evident. The problem is, however, that many are simply unaware of the progress we can make as a society by passing common-sense legislation and allowing businesses encompassed in these sectors the opportunity to flourish. By getting our apparel to the masses we hope to spread the message that reform is necessary like wildfire. In doing so, we also aspire to tear down the present barriers companies face and promote our cause of creating a climate that is friendlier towards all businesses involved in hemp, cannabis, and cryptocurrency.

www.topshelftoker.com

PROOF OF WORK (PoW) MINING

Proof of work mining is a competitive computerised process which helps to maintain and secure the blockchain in such a way as to verify transactions and prevent double spending.

In the general sense of cryptocurrency, those who participate in the activity of mining are called miners. They are general members of the cryptocurrency community who dedicate processing power (hash) of their computers towards solving highly complex mathematical problems and verifying transactions. This process upholds the integrity and security of the network. As such, miners are described as protectors of the network. Each transaction (held within a certain block) is validated before adding it to the blockchain. By doing this, they are rewarded (as an incentive) with newly generated mined coins or transaction fees. These coins are issued by the software in a transparent and predictable way outside of the control of its founders and developers. A miner can be based anywhere in the world as long as they have an internet connection, sufficient knowledge of how one mines and the hardware/software required to do so.

Miners use GPUs (Graphical Processing Units) or CPUs (Central Processing Units) to process transactions by hashing. Also, Application Specific Integrated Circuits (ASICs) allow miners to use customised hardware for faster and lower power mining.

Sativacoin was hybrid PoW/PoS for the first five days of its existence. It then became pure proof of stake on the 26th September 2014. Users of the desktop wallet client can earn up to 5% interest per annum on held coins. Proof of stake (PoS) is regarded as more environmentally friendly than proof of work.

BLOCKCHAIN

Every cryptocurrency has a corresponding blockchain within its decentralised network protocol. Sativacoin is no different in this sense. A blockchain is simply described as a general public ledger of all transactions and blocks ever executed since the very first block. In addition, it continuously updates in real time each time a new block is successfully mined. Blocks enter the blockchain in such a manner that each block contains the hash of the previous one. It is therefore utterly resistant to modification along the chain since each block is related to the prior one. Consequently, the problem of doubling-spending is solved.

As a means for the general public to view the blockchain, web developers have designed and implemented block explorers. They tend to present different layouts, statistics and charts. One of the best known block explorers for Sativacoin is:

* https://chainz.cryptoid.info/stv/

Some are more extensive in terms of the information given. Usual statistics included are:

* **Height of block** —the block number of the network.

* **Time of block** —the time at which the block was timestamped to the blockchain.

* **Transactions** —the number of transactions in that particular block.

* **Total Sent** —the total amount of cryptocurrency sent in that particular block.

* **Block Reward** —how many coins were generated in the block (added to the overall coin circulation).

BLOCK TIME

The block time is the average time taken for the network to successfully generate a certain block either by proof of work or proof of stake. Both the reward per block and the time of block generation dictate how the circulation of coins grows over time.

Official documentation states the average time for a block to be timestamped to the blockchain as sixty seconds. By taking into consideration the blocks below, the average time of a block during the first and second years can be calculated.

During the first year, a total of 426,799 blocks were timestamped. This equates to an average block time of 73.9 seconds for that period.

During the second year, a total of 409,508 blocks were timestamped. This equates to an average block time of 77.2 seconds for that period.

Block #1 (Reward 972 STV) September 21st 2014 at 04:09:57 PM UTC

Block #426,799 (Reward 0.0132715 STV) September 21st 2015 at 04:09:13 PM UTC

Block #426,800 (Reward 0.02910984 STV) September 21st 2015 at 04:10:42 PM UTC

Block #836,307 (Reward 0.01800384 STV) September 21st 2016 at 04:03:38 PM UTC

Block #836,308 (Reward 0.00540128 STV) September 21st 2016 at 04:10:22 PM UTC

CRYPTOCURRENCY EXCHANGES

A cryptocurrency exchange is a site on which registered users can buy or sell Sativacoin against Bitcoin, Litecoin, Dogecoin and so on. Some exchanges require users to fully register by submitting certain documentation including proof of identity and address. On the other hand, most exchanges only require users to register with a simple username and password with the use of a currently held e-mail account.

As well as being the method by which people can buy or sell STV, exchanges serve the purpose of setting the value of the coin. One unit of STV account has always been valued in terms of Bitcoin Satoshi (1 BTC Sat = 0.00000001 BTC). A direct trade between fiat (USD, GBP, EUR) and Sativacoin was available on C-Cex (USD). The STV/USD trading pair on C-Cex no longer exists.

At the time of book publication, three recognised cryptocurrency exchanges offered active trading of Sativacoin. These were Cryptopia, YoBit and Novaexchange.

Nine exchanges have supported trades of the coin. As can be seen below, six trading pairs are still active on three exchanges.

EXCHANGE	STATUS
Coinbroker	No longer supports STV
C-Cex	No longer supports STV
Bittrex	No longer supports STV
ALTS.trade	No longer supports STV
YoBit	STV/BTC
Cryptopia	STV/BTC, STV/LTC and STV/DOGE
Coingather	No longer supports STV
alcurEX	No longer supports STV
Novaexchange	STV/BTC and STV/DOGE

SATIVACOIN COMMUNITY

A community is a social unit or network that shares common values and goals. It derives from the Old French word "comuntee". This, in turn, originates from "communitas" in Latin (communis; things held in common). Sativacoin has a community consisting of an innumerable number of individuals who have the coin's well being and future goal at heart. These individuals almost always prefer fictitious names with optional corresponding "avatars". At the moment, there is one key figure of the project. He is called Arnel Larracas.

At the time of publication, there are social media sites (and other official websites) on which discussion and development of Sativacoin take place. These are:

Bitcointalk: https://bitcointalk.org/index.php?topic=1626516.0

Facebook: https://www.facebook.com/Sativacoin/

Official Website: https://www.sativacoin.io/

Twitter: https://twitter.com/arnie_barnie23

There have been two other Bitcointalk forum threads on which the coin has been discussed:

Previous thread: https://bitcointalk.org/index.php?topic=874071.0

Original thread: https://bitcointalk.org/index.php?topic=791266.0

There are plans to create an independent forum for Sativacoin.

In essence, the community surrounding and participating in the development of Sativacoin is the backbone of the coin. Without a following, the prospects of future adoption and utilisation are starkly limited. Sativacoin belongs to all those who use it, not just to the developers who aid its progression.

A CONCISE HISTORY OF SATIVACOIN

LIST OF CHAPTERS

1 —LAUNCH OF THE SATIVACOIN BLOCKCHAIN

2 —TAKEOVER OF SATIVACOIN BY
THE ALTCOIN.CENTER

3 —SATIVACOIN REBRANDED AND FORKED

4 —ALL TIME HIGH 2016 MARKET CAPITALISATION

5 —THIRD SATIVACOIN BITCOINTALK
FORUM THREAD CREATED

I.   BLOCKCHAIN LAUNCHED ON THE 21ST SEPTEMBER 2014

II. PROOF OF WORK ENDED ON THE 26TH SEPTEMBER 2014

III. COINBROKER, C-CEX AND BITTREX INITIATED STV TRADING

IV. EFFORTS MADE TO HIRE A NEW LEAD DEVELOPER

V.   STV ADDED TO WWW.COINMARKETCAP.COM

1

LAUNCH OF THE SATIVACOIN

BLOCKCHAIN

"With strong plans this coin could be a winner."

—user "SecondsOld"

When the founder of a cryptocurrency or development team decides to launch a blockchain, s/he usually proceeds by creating an official Bitcointalk thread. This was the case with Sativacoin. It was announced at 16:40:08 UTC on the 21st September 2014 as a X-13 (hashing algorithm) PoW/PoS (timestamping algorithm) coin. A user fictitiously know as "sativacoin" created a thread titled "[ANN] Sativacoin | STV | X-13 | NINJA LAUNCH". Within less than one minute, user "SecondsOld" was the first Bitcointalk forum member to respond. His comment is quoted immediately below the chapter title above.

Less than one hour before the original Sativacoin Bitcointalk forum thread was created, the first block had been timestamped. To be specific, the first nine blocks were timestamped before the announcement of the coin.

Block #1 (Reward 972 STV) September 21st 2014 at 04:09:57 PM UTC

Initial supporters of Sativacoin were quick to suggest, design and implement services for the coin. An IRC Chatroom was established to give the community a platform on which to discuss relevant social or technical topics. It was set up at https://kiwiirc.com/client/irc.freenode.net/sativacoin by user "najzenmajsen". Unfortunately, user "sativacoin" did not have time to immediately join it . User "sativacoin" had promised to release a roadmap of upcoming tasks and events. An enthusiastic quote by user "jimlite" on the 21st of September at 19:32:07 UTC was:

"Nice ninja launch, glad I got there with IPO miner. Hoping you guys update the ann with all the usual stuff to attract new miners, merchants, exchanges, twitter, facebook, etc."

One social media account at https://twitter.com/sativacoins was created on the 21st September. There were very few tweets posted by the account.

On the following day, Coinbroker was the first exchnage to initiate active trading of the coin at https://coinbroker.io/trade/?symbol=STV.BTC. There were initially problems with depositing and withdrawing STV on the site. User "sativacoin" contacted the exchange to resolve the issue, but received no response.

Coinbroker went live on the 10th February 2014. It originally supported BTC/LTC/PPC/NVC/DOGE at launch. They closed their doors on the 15th April 2016.

Forum users wanted to see the coin on C-Cex. They viewed it as a more highly reputable exchange which would serve the coin better in the long term. This became reality on the 22nd September as two separate trading pairs STV/BTC and STV/USD were initiated. C-Cex has been operational for over three years. Sativacoin is no longer present on the exchange.

C-CEX
CRYPTO-CURRENCY EXCHANGE

On the 23rd September, user "ShadowBits" was concerned about the time of the initial PoW phase of mining. He thought it was too short. As a result, the distribution of the total 6,998,400 STV (7,200 blocks) would be held in few hands. Accusations of an instamine (when coins are mined quickly before others can) were put forward. This was counteracted by user "ipominer" who said:

"There wasn't any substantial instamine. Let's be realistic, 9 blocks just does not matter at all, and the first blocks on a coin will always be mined in less than a few seconds. Even if the developer is using even a single GPU to start the blockchain, that's what you'll see. That's not an "instamine" by any stretch of the imagination though."

Bittrex was the third exchange (late UTC) to initiate the STV/BTC trading pair on the 23rd September. They are based in Seattle, WA and fully regulated in the United States of America. They began operations on the 13th February 2014 in beta testing mode. On the 28th February 2014, twelve cryptocurrencies went live as trading became active.

https://www.bittrex.com/Market/?MarketName=BTC-STV

Bittrex was the major trading platform for Sativacoin for over two years. There were periods during which time trading was deactivated due to very low daily volumes. Trading totally ceased on the platform on the 16th April 2017.

After the addition to Bittrex, user "sativacoin" was happy to say that only two days remained until the end of the proof of work mining phase. On the 24th September at 01:04:27 UTC, he stated that block number 3,329 had just been timestamped. He encouraged supporters of Sativacoin to join the IRC Chatroom. Initial Bitcoin Satoshi values of one unit of STV account on Bittrex were:

	Price	Low	Open	Close	High
23rd September 2014	750.5	501	1,000	501	1,000

On the 25th September, there was unfortunate news for those involved with the project. The lead developer, who had remained truly anonymous and behind the scenes, had abandoned Sativacoin. He felt discouraged by the abusive comments he had been receiving. User "sativacoin", who was the community voice of the coin, set out to hire a new lead developer. He viewed this as a hindrance to the future prospects of the coin, but not the end of it. Any suggestions on how to move forward were welcome. As time drew near to the end of proof of work mining after block number 7,200, user "sativacoin" was confident of Sativacoin becoming the biggest cannabis related coin in the crypto space.

On the following day at 21:58:31 UTC, the initial proof of work mining phase ended. A total of 6,998,400 STV had been mined in 7,200 blocks.

Block #7,200 (Reward 972 STV) September 26th 2014 at 09:58:31 PM UTC

Block #7,201 (Reward 0.27990309 STV) September 26th 2014 at 10:01:04 PM UTC

User "sativacoin" was quoted as saying:

"Pow stage is now over, and we have successfully entered Pos stage.

I am working on finding a new dev for the project, if you are a dev and wants to join the team pm me here or join irc channel #sativacoin at freenode."

Efforts were still being made to hire a competent and skilled lead developer who could help take the coin forward. As the month of September came to a close, disappointment was evident in terms of whether or not Savitacoin was being taken seriously.

On the 1st October at 03:24:44 UTC, user "popcorn75" said:

"Lets open a developer fund address and get this coin moving....
Any devs want to take this over?"

Block #14,199 (Reward 0.3960499 STV) October 1st 2014 at 11:26:05 PM UTC

On the 1st October, the number of STV generated since the launch of the blockchain surpassed 7,000,000 at block number 14,199.

Part of the community insisted upon a takeover of the coin. User "sativacoin" asked for patience as he was in the process of talking with a well known crypto developer. He was awaiting a response from him/her. At this point, user "sativacoin" was resilient and committed to stay with the coin. The original lead developer had hired him as the community manager.

On the 5th October, user "sativacoin" was still awaiting a response from the developer he had recently contacted four days ago. A significant and growing number of people gave their opinion. He said there was no reason to buy the coin if no plan existed. Shockingly, the last known post from user "sativacoin" was at 17:53:28 UTC on this same day:

"waiting for answers from dev i have contacted"

On the 20th October, twenty eight days after active trading commenced on Coinbroker, Sativacoin was added to www.coinmarketcap.com. It is a well known website to cryptocurrency supporters which lists hundreds of cryptocurrencies in order of market capitalisation (the total value of all units of account of a particular coin), daily trading volume or other statistics.

Two days later, user "Pastafarian" posted his first comment on the original Sativacoin Bitcointalk thread. He wanted to know if there had been any recent news. At 06:06:48 UTC on the 22nd of October, he was quoted as saying:

"Definitely a cheap coin in comparison to the others, so i had to pick some up. Hopefully the dev appears or a community takeover occurs so that the price can get to a more desirable level though!"

Throughout the following weeks, committed members of the community were deliberating about possible takeovers.

I.   SATIVACOIN TAKEN OVER ON THE 26TH NOVEMBER 2014

II.   A SECOND BITCOINTALK THREAD WAS CREATED

III.   SATIVACOIN ADDED TO PAYMENT PROVIDER COINTOPAY

IV.   NEW YEARS MESSAGE FROM ARNEL LARRACAS

V.   ALTS.TRADE INITIATED THE TRADING PAIR STV/BTC

2

TAKEOVER OF SATIVACOIN BY THE ALTCOIN.CENTER

"I hereby announce the takeover of SativaCoin by Altcoin.Center."

On the 26th November at 13:06:01 UTC, the Sativacoin community were made aware that a third party had taken over the coin. They were called the Altcoin.center, but no longer exist. They were tasked to provide the necessary updates to the wallet client, initiate the search of a lead developer and co-ordinate the social aspects of the coin. Their main responsibility was to look after the coin by doing their utmost to, in their own words, give it a long, stable and prosperous life. They charged 0.03 BTC per month for their service, but it was unknown who paid for it.

Without too much delay, a new official (second) Sativacoin Bitcointalk thread was created on the same day at 13:08:27 UTC titled "[ANN] [STV] SativaCoin TAKEOVER by Altcoin.Center - New official thread!" by the Altcoin.center. A Finnish individual called Jyri was in charge of the group.

Despite the coin being active on three exchanges, user "Pastafarian" (Arnel Larracas) had been busy tweeting other exchanges including Bter, HitBTC, Kraken, Poloniex, BTC-e and Cryptsy. At the time, these were some of the major trading platforms. He wanted as much help as possible to get Sativacoin on those.

Arnel Larracas was reaching out to people in the original Sativacoin Bitcointalk thread who had overlooked the creation of the new thread. He emphasised his commitment towards making the coin the leading cryptocurrency of the marijuana (cannabis) sector. Merchants, exchanges and other services were considering to adopt the coin. He viewed it as an opportunity not to be missed.

Arnel Larracas @arnie_barnie23 · 10 Dec 2014
Sativacoin (STV)...a quality pos coin with a bright future! #altcoins #btc #crypto

A few days before Christmas Day 2014, Arnel Larracas announced that Sativacoin had been added to https://cointopay.com. He provided the necessary funding to make this a reality. Cointopay is a payment provider that allows merchant services to receive payments in STV for their goods/services online.

Arnel Larracas, who had now become the leading figure of the coin, said:

"As 2015 nears here in Chicago, I must say that I am grateful to all who have supported and continue to support this project. Together we will silence those who criticize STV, especially since they have no basis for their argument."

On New Year's Day, a tweet on the official Sativacoin Twitter account read:

Arnel Larracas @arnie_barnie23 · 1 Jan 2015
Happy New Year Sativacoin (STV) community! Together we'll become the most trusted and valuable crypto for mj :) #btc #cannabis #pot #mj #420

It is well known how many scams exist within the crypto sphere. Nonetheless, the sphere is an exponentially growing market of promise, innovation and inspiration. Arnel Larracas knew that only the best coins would last. He was committed to see Sativacoin grow to the next level by inviting people to join the project. He was quoted as saying:

"The one promise that I can make is that I will work my hardest on this project. I never made a claim that STV was the most innovative coin either, but it is a reliable and quality pos coin. With our community takeover only taking effect recently, it seems as if you haven't even given us a chance to prove ourselves."

On the 6th January, ALTS.trade was the fourth exchange to initiate live trading of Sativacoin against Bitcoin. Their official Twitter announced the addition:

ALTS.Trade @ALTSTrade · 6 Jan 2015
STV/BTC #SativaCoin market added:
alts.trade/trade/STV/BTC
@AllCryptoAllDay

Over the next couple of months, Arnel Larracas was working on bridging the gap between the cryptocurrency sphere and the marijuana world, trying to create new merchant services and other plans behind the scenes to increase Sativacoin adoption. After several scares of being delisted, Sativacoin was still active on Bittrex. On the 28th February, according to www.coinmarketcap.com, the US Dollar values of one unit of STV account were:

	Price	Low	Open	Close	High
28th February 2015	0.000155	0.000153	0.000154	0.000155	0.000155

Other events which occurred during this period were:

- On the 14th December, Arnel Larracas suggested the coin needed a brand new logo. He offered a 10,000 STV bounty for the best design.

- On the 23rd January, an online shop at https://cryptoshop.altcoin.center/ began to accept STV as a method of payment. It went live ten days before this. It has since ceased to exist.

I.   HARD FORK OCCURRED ON THE 14TH MARCH 2015

II.   OFFICIAL WEBSITE CREATED AT WWW.SATIVACOIN.IO

III.   WORLDWIDE CELEBRATION OF CANNABIS CONSUMPTION

IV.   BITTREX TERMINATED STV/BTC TRADES FOR FOUR MONTHS

V.   YOBIT AND CRYPTOPIA BOTH INITIATED STV/BTC TRADING

3

SATIVACOIN REBRANDED AND HARD FORKED

"We have successfully forked STV and have control over the github. There are also new wallets that have been made for both mac and windows " — Arnel Larracas

Collaborations with third parties were still being deliberated upon as the month of March began. On the 2nd March, Arnel Larracas posted a small update about recent progress. He had been reaching out to developers from other cryptocurrencies to add value to Sativacoin. He planned to get the Windows and Mac OS X wallet clients updated as soon as possible.

In addition, he was trying to create a platform for STV to be traded against BTC and USD. He admitted he did not have the technical expertise to go ahead with the endeavour, so was looking for help. A substantial proportion of STV was set aside to fund it.

Also, a brand new coin logo design now existed. As can be seen on page number 34, it was described as more relevant than the original one. It is unknown who designed it or how it was chosen.

On the 14th March at 18:33:28 UTC, Arnel Larracas posted the following:

"We have successfully forked STV and have control over the github. There are also new wallets that have been made for both mac and windows

url source of github https://github.com/NewSativacoinDev/sativacoin
mac wallet https://mega.co.nz/#!9hRkUTCA!L70f0WgJ7i7S4mCnfXNoHNCLdwkOFInrNMTQ_vXTqN8
win wallet https://mega.co.nz/#!44l1DLDD!ZpObjzxOSX8Dr4iX3uNgLUOSMvJ1ud6MEusyOlVUQKl

Let's get the ball rolling for 4/20."

An official Facebook page was created at https://www.facebook.com/Sativacoin/ on 15th March. Members of the community were welcome to join this new social media group on which news updates would be regularly posted.

SativaCoin - STV
March 15 2015 ⓒ

Welcome to the official Facebook page for Sativacoin!

Following on from the publication of the new coin logo, an "Accepted Here" graphic was also unveiled. It was made freely available to any merchants who had adopted Sativacoin as a means of payment for their goods/services.

One particular promotion was active during the month of April. Official Sativacoin clothing was on sale (free shipping). Supporters of the coin could now celebrate the 20th April in crypto style (www.teespring.com/sativacoin?pr=FR33SHIP). The free shipping lasted until the 23rd April.

On the 19th July, Bittrex terminated the STV/BTC trading pair on their exchange. As a result of the exchange being the only recognised one trading STV, the website www.coinmarketcap.com could no longer collect data to calculate the market capitalisation and other statistics. A historical chart below shows how the market capitalisation fluctuated from the 20th October 2014 to the 19th July 2015. A peak was attained on the 11th April. At that peak, the market capitalisation was recorded at approximately US$7,000. One unit of STV account stood at roughly US$0.001 or 429 Bitcoin Satoshi. However, the Bitcoin Satoshi value of one STV had been above 429 before (23rd September 2014) on Bittrex. What follows are the Bitcoin Satoshi values of one unit of STV account leading up to the 11th April 2015:

	Price	Low	Open	Close	High	Volume (STV)
7th April	141	113	156	126	182	63,287.27
9th April	232	214	232	232	232	41,273.01
11th April	165	65	200	130	429	202,148.8

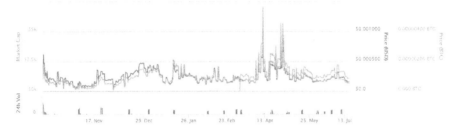

On the 21st September, as soon as block number 426,800 had been timestamped, the blockchain was one year old. A total of 7,035,749.62536595 STV had been generated since mining/minting began (6,998,400 STV mined in 7,200 PoW blocks).

Block #1 (Reward 972 STV) September 21st 2014 at 04:09:57 PM UTC

Block #426,799 (Reward 0.0132715 STV) September 21st 2015 at 04:09:13 PM UTC

Block #426,800 (Reward 0.02910984 STV) September 21st 2015 at 04:10:42 PM UTC

On the 17th November, YoBit was the fifth exchange to list STV for active trading. It is an exchange based in Russia and went live on the 5th January 2015.

SativaCoin [STV] is listed: https://yobit.net/en/trade/STV/BTC
SativaCoin Dice: https://yobit.net/en/dice/STV
Donate STV coins to our Giveaway: https://yobit.net/en/freecoins/
Please report about STV update/fork/issue here: https://yobit.net/en/reportupdate/STV

On the following day, news broke that Bittrex had reopened the STV/BTC trading pair at https://bittrex.com/Market/Index?MarketName=BTC-STV. Members of the community rejoiced at the news. On the next day, www.coinmarketcap.com relisted Sativacoin. Arnel got so motivated that he tweeted other exchanges such as CCEDK, Poloniex and Bleutrade to see if they would consider trades of STV.

On the 10th December, two days after winning the exchange vote, seven trading pairs opened on the Cryptopia exchange. Arnel happily announced these pairs:

Sativacoin/Bitcoin https://www.cryptopia.co.nz/Exchange?market=STV_BTC

Sativacoin/Dotcoin https://www.cryptopia.co.nz/Exchange?market=STV_DOT

Sativacoin/Litecoin https://www.cryptopia.co.nz/Exchange?market=STV_LTC

Sativacoin/Dogecoin https://www.cryptopia.co.nz/Exchange?market=STV_DOGE

Sativacoin/Feathercoin https://www.cryptopia.co.nz/Exchange?market=STV_FTC

Sativacoin/Popularcoin https://www.cryptopia.co.nz/Exchange?market=STV_POP

Sativacoin/Unobtanium https://www.cryptopia.co.nz/Exchange?market=STV_UNO

Cryptopia launched on the 6th December 2014. Its official website describes it as:

"Cryptopia, written from scratch and designed from the ground up to be a by the users for the users one stop hub for all things cryptocurrency related. We believe that in order for cryptocurrencies to become widely adopted and prosper they need to be easily accessible, user friendly, and above all usable for actual goods and services. We aim to not just be another exchange, but to innovate and focus on the user experience, and ultimately make cryptocurrencies more accessible to everyone.

Cryptopia Limited is an incorporated LLC in New Zealand."

It was clear that development of the coin had been hampered throughout the year of 2015. Nevertheless, Arnel was fully devoted to making Sativacoin a long term success. He wanted to deliver rather than just talk. He looked forward to 2016.

Other events which occurred during this period were:

- On the 20th March, another block explorer was announced as being live at http://blockexperts.com/stv.

- On the 11th December, the account https://twitter.com/sativacoinbot was founded.

- On the 16th December, Cryptocloud Hosting began to accept STV on their platform at https://cryptocloudhosting.org/

₿ 0.00004200 - ALL TIME STV - BTC HIGH!

The highest daily close for the STV - BTC pair - ₿ 0.00004200 was recorded on Thursday, 01 September 2016. It has not been as expensive (or cheap, depending on how much you love STV) since.

I. **COINGECKO BEGAN TO STATISTICALLY RANK SATIVACOIN**

II. **COINPAYMENTS.NET ADDED SATIVACOIN**

III. **COINGATHER, ALCUREX AND NOVAEXCHANGE ADDED STV**

IV. **LOWEST 2016 BTC VALUE OF ONE STV RECORDED**

V. **ALL TIME HIGH 2016 MARKET CAPITALISATION RECORDED**

4

ALL TIME HIGH 2016
MARKET CAPITALISATION

"Happy New Year everyone!!! 2016 has a lot in store for Sativacoin and I am looking forward to continuing the tremendous progress we have made." — Arnel Larracas

As is evident above, Arnel Larracas was enthusiastic about the future prospects of Sativacoin. It would ultimately depend on user adoption and how the coin could be utilised by its users.

On the 3rd January, the seventh cryptocurrency exchange initiated live trading of Sativacoin against Bitcoin at https://www.coingather.com/exchange/STV/BTC. As with other exchanges, Arnel Larracas thanked Coingather for the addition.

After thirteen months of coding (284 builds, 872 revisions), the exchange was proudly announced as live on the 31st July 2014. They reached a 500 registered user mark on the 6th April 2016. They are viewed as a minor exchange. Sativacoin is no longer active on Coingather.

On the 5th January, Sativacoin was integrated into the website called CoinGecko. It is a cryptocurrency valuation and ranking website. They help to quantitatively evaluate and rank coins.

On the 3rd July 2017, the top ten cryptocurrencies ranked on CoinGecko were:

Coin	Development	Community	Public Interest	Total
Bitcoin, BTC	98	93	99	97
Ethereum, ETH	93	74	89	91
Litecoin, LTC	89	66	46	80
Ripple, XRP	78	57	62	76
Monero, XMR	85	54	46	70
Dash, DASH	79	50	49	69
Zcash, ZEC	88	37	55	69
Siacoin, SC	85	51	44	68
Golem, GNT	84	49	52	68
Dogecoin, DOGE	72	65	46	67

CoinGecko
@coingecko

Following

(1/2) New coins added to CoinGecko:

BitCrystals (BCY)
Amsterdamcoin (AMS)
Synereo (AMP)
Aeon (AEON)
Digicube (CUBE)
Sativacoin (STV)

Two weeks later on the 19th January, the eighth exchange initiated live trading of Sativacoin at https://alcurex.org/index.php/crypto/market?pair=STV_BTC. It is an online cryptocurrency financing company registered in Finland. It launched on the 7th June 2014 after months of beta testing.

Officially recognised websites on which Sativacoin could be found and used were:

EXCHANGES

https://bittrex.com/Market/Index?MarketName=BTC-STV
https://alcurex.org/index.php/crypto/index
https://www.cryptopia.co.nz/Exchange?market=STV_BTC
(plus other trading pairs at Cryptopia inc. LTC, DOGE)
https://yobit.net/en/trade/STV/BTC
https://www.coingather.com/exchange/STV/BTC
https://coinbroker.io/trade/?symbol=STV.BTC
https://alts.trade/trade/STV/BTC

CHARTS/PRICE TRACKING

https://twitter.com/SativaCoinBot
http://coinmarketcap.com/currencies/sativacoin/
http://www.worldcoinindex.com/coin/sativacoin
http://coincap.io/#/coin/stv
https://www.coingecko.com/en/coins/sativacoin

OTHER OFFICIAL WEBSITES

http://www.sativacoin.io/
https://twitter.com/arnie_barnie23
https://www.facebook.com/Sativacoin/
https://github.com/NewSativacoinDev/sativacoin
http://stv.explorer.bitnodes.net/

On the 25th March, Arnel Larracas posted on the official STV Bitcointalk thread after just over two months absence of posting. He was quoted as saying:

"A big thanks to everyone that has continued to support Sativacoin! I have not put out any news since I'd like to deliver first but know that I am still here. I was so happy to see that we have been trading in the 700 satoshi range on Bittrex. While we have made a lot of progress thus far though, this is only the beginning. May we continue our journey toward becoming the premier coin for cannabis and hemp."

On the annual celebration (20th April) of the consumption of cannabis and hemp, Arnel issued an important update. He said he had been working tirelessly to make this update a reality. Coinpayments.net had just made the following announcement on Twitter:

CoinPayments @CoinPaymentsNET · 20 Apr 2016
😛 Perfect day to start accepting payments using #SativaCoin via @CoinPaymentsNET Sativacoin - STV -... fb.me/728z81o4t

Arnel Larracas notified the community that the official Sativacoin Bitcointalk thread had been read over 40,000 times. He described the trading of the coin as strong, word was spreading quickly and, as he continued his quest to make Sativacoin the premier digital currency for hemp and cannabis, it looked to be the best 4/20 yet.

Also on the 20th April, the Bitcoin Satoshi value of one unit of STV account surpassed 1,000 for the first time. Values derived from Bittrex were:

	Price	Low	Open	Close	High	STV Volume
20th April	1,020	802	833	1,207	1,226	101,008.59

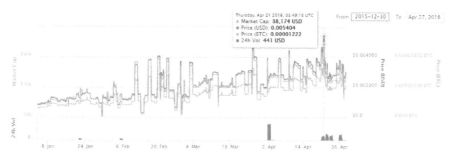

Two days later, the ninth exchange called Novaexchange began to offer active trading of STV against BTC at https://novaexchange.com/market/BTC_STV/. They are based in Sweden and went live (beta) eighteen days before adding STV/BTC.

Novaexchange @nova_exchange · 4 Apr 2016
Novaexchange is open for closed beta! A few markets online! Help finding bugs and problems, sign up and try! novaexchange.com

Two milestone events which occurred during May were:

- A paper wallet service was made available for people to easily stash away Sativacoin. It is hosted at http://dev.cryptolife.net/paperwallet/sativacoin/

- On the 8th May, Cryptopia opened the STV/ETH trading pair (Ethereum, ETH) at https://www.cryptopia.co.nz/Exchange/?market=STV_ETH

On the 16th June, the lowest value of one unit of STV account during 2016 was recorded at 106 Bitcoin Satoshi. The market capitalisation fell below US$6,000.

On the 1st September, the all time high market capitalisation of 2016 was reached at approximately US$169,861. There had been immense volatility over the summer. At the time of publication of the book, the Bitcoin Satoshi value has not yet surpassed the high of 4,200 or the corresponding market capitalisation high.

Thursday, Sep 01 2016, 23:34:14 UTC
Market Cap: 169,861 USD
Price (USD): 0.024023
Price (BTC): 0.00004200
24h Vol: 2 USD

During the penultimate week of September, Arnel Larracas was looking for as much help as possible with the coin, especially on the technical side of things. He was looking to put together a team to oversee the source code and continue development. Being based in the US near Chicago was viewed as a bonus. Investors were being sought to support the project.

Other events which occurred during this period were:

- On the 9th January, a faucet (free source of small amounts of STV) was created at the URL http://sillypothead.com/stvfaucet.

- On the 27th April, Pex Peppers (described as hot sauce) became the first CoinPayments.net merchant to accept Sativacoin (see image opposite).

I.   NEW BITCOINTALK THREAD CREATED ON THE 25TH SEP 2016

II.   TRANSLATIONS OF STV BITCOINTALK INTO OTHER LANGUAGES

III.   SATIVACOIN WAS ACTIVE ON FOUR EXCHANGES ON 1ST OCT

IV.   HIGHEST 2016 DAILY VOLUME RECORDED ON 13TH OCTOBER

V.   LAST BLOCK OF 2016 TIMESTAMPED AT 23:59:44 UTC

5

THIRD SATIVACOIN BITCOINTALK FORUM THREAD CREATED

"Well the premine occurred under the previous dev so I never saw the $25 haha. I can also assure everyone that I have spent far more than that on development anyways ."
— user "Pastafarian"

Enthusiasm for Sativacoin evidently waned during the summer. As a result, Arnel created a new Bitcointalk forum thread for the coin on the 25th September 2016 at 02:45:39 UTC at "[ANN] SativaCoin (STV)-The Cryptocurrency Built For Hemp and Cannabis-Est. 2014". Its prime purpose was to breathe new life into the coin.

Arnel Larracas was asked a question: "What is the difference between Potcoin and Sativacoin?". Arnel answered on the 27th September at 19:35:06 UTC by saying:

"To answer your question simply, a significant difference is the number of coins. As of this writing there are 7,070,740 STV vs. 214,257,330 POT.

To answer your question with a little more complexity though, I have a fundamentally different vision for SativaCoin. Furthermore, I have access to many helpful tools and people that will benefit STV in the long run "

As promised earlier, a new block explorer went live on the 27th September at https://chainz.cryptoid.info/stv/.

Over the next few days of September, the opening post (OP) of the official Sativacoin Bitcointalk thread was translated into other languages. These were:

- User "killerjoegreece" posted the Greek version on the 28th September

- User "Coin_trader" posted the Filipino translation on the 28th September

- User "Woshib" posted the French translation on the 28th September

- User "forummaster" posted the Italian translation on the 29th September

- User "freemind1" posted the Spanish translation on the 29th September

- User "ShooterXD" posted the Portuguese translation on the 29th September

Arnel Larracas thanked the users above who had provided a translation. They were all subsequently listed on the OP. He was also happy to announce that the official website www.sativacoin.io had been completely redesigned in order to make it look more professional and appealing to visitors. Some users asked whether Arnel would consider a signature campaign. Arnel responded by saying he would post an update if one begins. A definition of a signature campaign is:

"A signature campaign is often organized by an individual, group or company who want to promote a certain coin, platform or service."

On the 1st October, Arnel reminded people that the timestamping algorithm is pure proof of stake. He was still trying to get the coin added to a multipool (miners mine other coins, but get paid in STV). At this time, he listed four active cryptocurrency exchanges on which STV was trading:

Cryptocurrency Exchange	Traded Against	Date Initiated
Bittrex	BTC	23/09/2014
Cryptopia	BTC, LTC, DOGE, FTC, POT, UNO, ETH	10/12/2015
YoBit	BTC	17/11/2015
Coingather	BTC	03/01/2016

On the 13th October, the highest daily STV/BTC trading volume for 2016 was recorded at 5.85 BTC. This happened during the 10th-16th week in which the highest weekly volume of 2016 was 13.15 BTC. The vast majority of the volume was due to trades at Bittrex (no longer active on this exchange). Corresponding BTC Satoshi and daily STV trading volumes on Bittrex are tabulated below. The data was derived from www.cryptocompare.com

	Price	Low	Open	Close	High	STV Volume
10th Oct	685	525	721	649	1,149	143,908.48
11th Oct	794	649	649	939	1,060	16,458.69
12th Oct	769.5	406	939	600	1,060	115,209.26
13th Oct	550.5	420	600	501	699	1,103,223.29
14th Oct	500.5	415	501	500	537	686,769.87
15th Oct	461.5	450	450	473	524	355,750.56
16th Oct	484.5	426	473	496	504	14,164.47

Taking into consideration an approximate value of Bitcoin at US$637 on the 13th October, one unit of STV account equated to roughly US$0.00351. This was more than triple the value of STV on the 11th April 2015.

Also in October, there were discussions of a possible Sativacoin Foundation. Arnel said it was on the "to-do" list. Anyone interested in being part of a foundation was asked to contact him. He wished for qualified individuals to oversee a foundation which would be responsible for the development and promotion of the coin.

As the end of 2016 drew near, the community were happy that Sativacoin was still active on Bittrex. There had been a few occasions the exchange warned of delisting the coin. As well as exchange activity, Arnel asked the community to reach out to merchants to accept the coin as a method of payment. Sativacoin was still present on the payment provider called Coinpayments.net.

Last block timestamped to the blockchain in 2016 was:

Block #895,326 (Reward 0.02448235 STV) December 31st 2016 at 11:59:44 PM UTC